HAPPY FATHERS DAY!

LOVE FROM ________

Made in the USA
Monee, IL
16 June 2022

98099252R10056